The Insider's Guide
to Extreme Interview

*How to Answer
Bizarre Questions*

Martha Gage

ISBN: 1724529188

CONTENTS

Introduction

The fact that you're reading this book suggests that the stakes are high. Perhaps you're anticipating an interview for your dream job. Whatever your situation, you recognize that impressing an interviewer is the next crucial step in your career.

You'll be relieved to know that being an impressive interviewee is an easy skill to master. You don't need physical strength or superior intellect. You need a strategy and time to practice. In this book, I'll give you a game plan. With this and with some practice, you can quickly learn how to give amazing interview answers and get offers for the jobs you want.

While interviewing hundreds of candidates over the years, I've seen interviews that fall into three categories. About 70% are disappointing. Unprepared candidates struggle through their interviews with answers that are either vague or don't address the questions I ask.

About 20% of the interviews are good. Candidates are prepared, and they respond to most questions with clear, relevant answers.

Finally, about 10% of the interviews are

amazing. These candidates answer every question with poise and confidence. Their responses are riveting, and I wish I could interview them for hours. This third group will breeze through life getting whatever jobs they want.

In this book, my goal is to help you be amazing in your future job interviews so you can be in that top 10%.

Most amazing candidates are not naturally gifted. They don't have superpowers that enable them to answer any question that they are asked. Their secret is preparation.

What a joy it will be when you complete interviews knowing that you nailed them. If you follow the steps in this book, you should experience that feeling every time you complete an interview.

You can also use these skills to be more persuasive in every aspect of your life. Not only do interview skills help you get the jobs you want, they help you persuade people to see your point of view in various situations. I haven't changed jobs in years, but I use my interview skills every day. I use them to get more resources at work, I use them to explain new concepts to my kids and I use them to give advice to friends.

This book is intended to be a workbook. I recommend you take notes as you read it, and write down your personalized answers to the interview questions.

Chapter 1

Demystifying Extreme Interviews

I would like you to think of the interview as a conversation between two people trying to get to know one another better. It's an opportunity for the employer:

- To explain the role and job description in more detail.

- To evaluate your skills relative to the job, your communication skills, how you think on your feet, your judgment and your personality and attitude.

- To describe future opportunities and maybe even discuss your potential career path, to see if you would be interested in joining them.

And it is a great opportunity for you:

- To expand the interviewer's understanding and appreciation of your skills. A one or two-page resume can't possibly capture the essence of who you are.

- To understand the company's culture—it could be laid back or more formal. Do they promote from within, and how do they treat their people? I always suggest arriving 15-20 minutes early so you can observe how employees interact in the reception area. Are they snarly with one another or are they supportive? Are they smiling and laughing? Does the company have values that match yours? Listen carefully as they discuss their mission and values with you.

- To determine whether you liked what you heard when they talked about their company and future opportunities. Are they a good match for you?

Many candidates think of an interviewer as an opponent. They think the interviewer is hoping they will fail. Nothing could be further from the truth. An interviewer is more like a reluctant judge in a contest. They're hoping to find someone who meets the criteria of the contest. Once they find a worthy candidate, they're happy to select that person and award them the prize of a job offer. That way, they can end the interview process. An interviewer wants you to succeed. They want you to win the contest so they can hire you and get back to their regular job.

Your goal should be to make it easy for the interviewer to select you as the contest winner. You want them to envision you in the role they are trying to fill. To do that, you should tailor your answers to the role. If the role requires creativity, you should highlight your creative skills. If the role requires organization, tell them how organized you are.

Most firms around the world are always carrying out the traditional in-person job interviews to decide which employees to hire. This does not work anymore, since this has become a tool in which most interviewees lie to be considered appropriate. People have become dishonest with their responses. Take a case where an interviewee is asked about a certain skill they don't possess. Knowing that if they admit to not having the skill they will lose the job, they will talk around it and provide that false impression.

With such important decisions, most employers are making use of extreme interviewing to test the ability of job seekers to think smartly and from their own point of imagination. It was a style initiated by one of the greatest pioneers - Steve Jobs, the cofounder of Apple - who used to position interviewees in a room and put them through their paces. The extreme interview consisted of three principles; drop the regular job interviews, involve the existing team and involve personality matters.

Steve Jobs applied the first principle of drop the regular job interview to create the work environment for the candidates, and with this interviewers could see candidates in a real working condition.

Involve the existing team. This works best since the co-workers will help to identify the most suitable partner to work with. If the human resource manager tends to hire the wrong candidate, then the problem will automatically affect the company and the co-workers.

Personality matters. This one usually focuses on technical skills and the personal skills that a candidate has. It is always good to prefer a candidate who has better communication skills and teamwork.

The reason why Steve Jobs liked using the extreme interview is that it was efficient when managing big interviews with few resources, and was consistent and congruent. It makes it easy to select new employees and to know the ones with the ability to fit in the position. It's radical, and it's the best technique since it works better than the traditional way.

There have been advances in extreme interviewing. Menlo Innovations, a software development firm based in Michigan, carry out extreme interviewing by alerting applicants that what they will encounter is not questions based on their resume, but an attempt to find the best fit to conform to the working culture of the firm. Menlo simulates the work environment by bringing 50 applicants at a time and pairing them for a session of 20 minutes. Exercises that are typical to the day to day operations of the firm are given to the candidates, as a staff member observes the interactions of the applicants. After 20 minutes, partners are swapped and new exercises and a different observer are given out. This is then done for a third time and the intention is to determine whether the candidate can bring the best qualities and make their partners perform at their best.

Goals for recruiting new employees by the use of extreme interviews

- To increase the productivity of the employees on the project thus increasing profits.

- To get new best professionals in the field and see how they can tackle problems.
- It is possible to progress with work while interviewing.
- It is the best way to think up new ideas.
- Supports teamwork.

A Sao Paulo based company also adopted the extreme interviews. They get all the applicants together, and the employees from Semco are the ones to carry out the interview session. It reveals a better way of hiring new employees in an organization.

Google Inc., Zappos and Hewlett-Packard are known to expose applicants to brain twisters. Candidates are asked tricky questions. These questions are usually made for testing their ability to think smart. Such questions do not have a right answer, but test the creativity of the job seekers and how they handle themselves when under pressure. So when interviewees are giving out the answers, they don't have to be correct but should always give a logical explanation.

In Los Angeles, the human resource teams mostly use extreme interviewing to select appropriate candidates to work. They are subjected to troubles or situations that can only be watched on a reality TV program like Survivor and The Apprentice reality shows.

Graduates who applied for various positions at Likeable Media, a social media marketing agency in New York, were told to explain why they should be selected to work for the company through Twitter social media. The questions were tweeted and candidates would answer by use of a common hashtag. Sometimes the candidates applying for the same job could meet near a restaurant to interact with one another to see how one can emerge the winner.

The Dos and Don'ts

Here are a few tips for all types of interview answers:

Do:

- **Be positive**: You should focus on the positive aspects of your experiences. Employers want to hire people who can be positive in any circumstance, so show them that you can do that.

- **Be passionate**: Employers want to hire people who really want to work. Show them that you enjoy the type of work that they are hiring for.

- **Be specific**: Employers want to hear specifically what you've done and the results you've personally delivered.

- **Be concise**: Your answers should be long enough to get the interviewer interested in you, but not so long that they think you're monopolizing the conversation. Most answers should be less than one minute, and you should never give an answer that takes more than two minutes.

- **Be grateful**: The interviewer is taking time out of their day to talk with you. Let them know that you appreciate their time and their consideration. You should start the interview by thanking them, end the interview by thanking them and send a thank you card or email after the interview.

- **Give examples**: There's a great saying: "Facts tell, but stories sell." People remember stories, so tell the interviewer stories about what you've done and what you've accomplished. The stories should be brief, but include enough detail that the interviewer can envision you in that situation.

- **Use frameworks**: In this book, I'll show you several useful frameworks that will help you structure your answers to any type of question. Using a framework will prevent you from rambling or being vague during interviews.

- **Be honest**: You should be truthful in every response. Not only is it the right thing to do, but interviewers often do their own fact-checking on their top candidates. If you say that you accomplished something and they find out you didn't, you could end your chances of ever working for that company.

Don't:

- **Don't be modest**: Interviews are not the place to be humble. You should proudly talk about your biggest accomplishments, your most relevant work experiences and any major awards you have won. Interviewers like to hear about results and accomplishments, and they love meeting confident candidates.

- **Don't be personal**: Don't talk about personal information such as family, friends and hobbies that are unrelated to the job. Don't talk about religion, politics, your favorite sports teams or any topics that could be polarizing.

- **Don't be negative**: No matter how bad any of your previous jobs or bosses has been, don't say anything bad about them during an interview.

- **Don't be verbose**: Don't go into too much detail in any specific area. As you practice your interview skills, find a brief way to answer each question so you're providing an amazing answer without repeating yourself or droning on with unnecessary details.

Chapter 2

The Unique Strategies in Extreme Interviews

Human resource departments nowadays have adopted the extreme interview methods when looking for candidates to hire. The interview is carried out by asking complex questions that are intended to make the candidate think outside the box. However, candidates are required to have potential skills and experience on their Curriculum Vitae to qualify for the next step. Candidates should also possess high thinking capacity and wonderful work habits to assist them in making the right decision. Those are some the most vital requirements that human resource managers usually look for in the interviewee, and if you have them it automatically provides you with a better platform to be interviewed and be selected.

To enable you to comprehend the new interviewing systems, here is a breakdown of every procedure.

Dinosaur Interviewing

Dinosaur interview technique is used to find out the best candidate who can think creatively and respond in the most fantastic way when under pressure. The name "Dinosaur Interview" was formed from the most famous question: "If you were a dinosaur, which would you be and why?" The big companies like HP and Google apply other challenging questions like rating your wittiness on a scale of 1 to 10 or summarizing the economy of the world in one word. These questions are aimed at challenging the interviewee to think of appropriate answers other than the commonly known responses or the commonly known dinosaur like T-Rex.

These questions have no right answers, but you have to be smart and logical in the way you approach them. The interviewee is requested to be well prepared by conducting dinosaur research with friends, to research the history of dinosaur interviewing and use the online interactive plan of Felch Quarry.

Candidates should then keep these questions in mind when responding. If a hiring human resource manager is challenging you on your creative thinking skills, you should probably decide to be a dinosaur.

Group Interviews

Group interviews consist of two main types - the first one is a panel group and the other one is candidate grouping.

In a panel interview, the interviewee will be interviewed by several interviewers in a single session. The interviewee is requested to be focused and to concentrate on all the interviewers in the panel. They should remain cool and not allow the board of interviewers to challenge them or get them off topic. Applicants are requested to adequately prepare themselves in a smart manner by practicing for the interview with a video or audio recorder - in this situation, be prepared to reveal a summary of who you are and your career objectives. Each panel member will ask you questions and then the panel will meet afterwards to determine who they believe is the best candidate. Please remember to look at all the panel members when answering questions, not just the member who asked you the specific question.

In a candidate group interviewing, one interviewer organizes the interview with many candidates at once. The main reason for holding the candidate group session is to get the best candidate who possesses the teamwork spirit, the one who can work under pressure, the one with advanced leadership skills and the one who is innovative.

During the interview, the candidates should be very keen when listening to the interviewer, to speak with a purpose to enable points to flow and to follow up with a thank you letter. Then always remember the basics rules of an interview that a candidate should have such as attractive appearance, promptness, dignity and loyalty as this will help any candidate stand out as the best candidate among the crowd. Evaluators will be looking for your leadership and communication abilities and observe how you work in a team. The group dilemma shows how you stand out compared to your peer candidates.

Presentation Interviews

Human resource personnel usually come up in the interview, then he/she will disclose the problem affecting the organization to the candidates who are present in the interview panel. Then it's upon the candidates to conduct serious research and investigations upon the problem. They are given an hour, two days or a one week period with appropriate resources and information to come up with a better solution to the organization's problem.

Candidates should maintain their exposure since they are only tested on their ability to come up with a solution, and give out the best way on how to solve the problem. They should use professional presentation aids and visual components that are specified in the organization. They should incorporate even the most cherished photos on their PowerPoint layout during the presentation. For example, if it is an interview for Google, it's better to integrate the presentation with their brand colors. Candidates should be accurate when presenting their facts by knowing who their audience is and how the information will be transmitted.

"Speed dating" - style interviews

Candidates are given approximately 15 minutes to introduce and market themselves to the interviewers. This helps human resource managers to go through a large number of applicants over a short span of time. Screening of applicants is done by use of modern technology equipment such as Skype, and the use of a smartphone.

Hirelite, an online recruitment platform, has embraced technology by enabling software engineers to be interviewed in five minutes by the use of video conferencing. Pizza Hut is another firm that has integrated speed interviewing in its culture using seemingly the best cutting-edge tactic; it only gives candidates 140 seconds to present and market themselves.

A speed dating interview is one of the ways to measure one's fitness. It reveals how we make a quick decision about a candidate in the first few minutes of an interview. In the first few minutes of an interview, interviewers should pay high attention to any brief information that is being disclosed by the candidate. These immediate impressions are very meaningful in matters concerned with best decision making. If nothing else, such interviews prompt people to have a close check for relevant information in the session.

Never be surprised when you attend a job interview thencome across these extreme interviewing techniques. Then it will be best to apply this knowledge in the interview to be able to predict what employers are looking for and position yourself on top of the competition.

Chapter 3

Categories of Questions

In an interview expect all sorts of questions, including strange questions. In this section, we categorize the strange questions into three groups.

Smart questions

The employer will have the desire to determine if you can think outside the box and help out when faced with unclear circumstances. The questions you will be asked are meant to test your ingenuity. You have to show that you are not the kind of individual who will always follow presets, but who will go out of the normal way to sort through various options and provide estimates. For instance, you may be asked about the number of red cars in a given city. Answer logically by estimating the population of the city and the proportion of people who own cars. Once you have the estimated number of car owners, allocate a percentage which will give an estimate of red. Do not respond by stating that you do not know.

Questions on stress resistance

These questions might be asked in order to see how you react to uncomfortable and unexpected situations, and whether you're able to stay cool and deal with difficult people.

The candidate is generally not told this technique will be used. So if you find yourself hearing questions like this, realize that it may be a test. First, smile and breathe. Think of it as an interesting challenge, maybe even a sort of game, to stay utterly calm and professional and give the best possible answer.

- "What do you do that drives your boss crazy?"
  (Answer that you don't do anything that drives your boss crazy, but that you're always looking to improve your skills.)

- "How would you evaluate me as an interviewer?"
  (How about "Very cautiously"! Beyond that, the correct answer depends on the job you're interviewing for.)

- "What's the worst thing you've heard about our   company?"
  (If something negative has appeared in the news or is well known, tactfully

acknowledge what you've seen and be prepared to discuss the issue and how you feel about it.)

How you behave in such a stressful instance, how you cope, your readiness to communicate correctly, and your knowledge towards providing a resolution to the situation without being offensive or humiliating another person will determine if you will get the job.

Questions "about nothing"

When you provide the obvious answers to the standard questions, the interviewer will want to hear something different from the rehearsed responses. These offbeat questions are usually targeted at you to check how well you are able to think on your feet. Remember, weird though they may seem, your responses to these questions reflect your core personality. So be extremely careful about how you answer them. An example of such a question is: If you were given an opportunity to turn into a beast, which would you choose and why?

There are no right answers and every answer has its own merits and demerits. Do not be unnerved by these kinds of queries. Take ample time to put your thoughts together and be assured something will pop in your head because you are already well prepared. However, be honest and do not exaggerate to the point of complete disbelief or show that your attitude reflects your casual approach to most things in life. Be realistic and come up with answers that are logical and make sense.

Chapter 4

The Successful Tactics

In the current setting, securing a job position is proving to be a hard task for every job seeker around. Many will feel very happy to have secured a chance for an interview invitation. They become cautious when they are in the interview room facing the interviewers. Playing safe is not a true reflection that will lead to getting the job. You need to embrace extreme interview tactics to have the upper hand and securing the position.

Here are some of the tactics you need to understand to be successful.

The Walkout

As a normal routine the interviewee is expected to walk into the room, sit down, stay calm in the process, allow the interviewers to scold the work and go home expecting a callback. The lucky ones would get the callback.

The walkout technique is a unique one applied when a hiring manager goes ahead to demonize and demean your work, calling it crap and showing that they are not impressed at all.

Having faced the same situation, I couldn't bear it and knew that there was no way I would be employed in this firm. I calmly stood up, closed my resume and politely thanked the hiring manager for the time accorded to me. I clearly showed that from their statements, my work did not suit the company.

Amazingly, as I walked out, the interviewer walked to me and assured me that it was a moment of trying to be harsh and that they knew that there were some strong aspects in my portfolio. It was just a test to determine how a candidate reacts to real situations of ego bashing. I won the job since the kind of reaction I exemplified was the one they needed the most. Always trust your gut when you have to react to some other unexpected situations.

The Pocket Surprise

When you go for an interview, always carry something in your pocket. Since you may not have attended an interview for a while, you may experience some nervousness. You will be hit by the last question in which the HR manager asks to know if you really fit in. It may be a small plastic cow or house that your kid gave to you. Solidly assure the manager that you have the object in your possession and set it on the table. There will be silence everywhere and they will then burst into laughter. Such an act makes the interviewer see you as a person and not a candidate and you will win the interview.

The Refusal

This is the most daring thing you can do. You know deep within you that you need the job but you go ahead and refuse the offer or something the interviewer requests you to do. This renders the interviewer powerless as they deemed that they were the ones in control.

The best approach is ensuring you are composed and take control of the interview. Do the unexpected but not to the extreme of having to be kicked out of the room for breaking state laws. Refuse requests and offers presented, and question every action to ensure that you stand out as a special candidate.

The Honest Approach

It is good to be honest with your answers. But remember that the interviewers are used to such answers and some of them can bring boorishness and upset them.

Do not give the interviewers much of clichéd answers. The truth, rather than a rehearsed response will impress the interviewer and will make you the most fit candidate for the position.

The Bluff

You may be presented with situations of solving hard problems or puzzles as presented by the interviewer. The first task may be familiar to you and you will tell the interviewer that you have faced the same puzzle before and go ahead to give the correct answer to the puzzle.

To handle puzzle questions:

- Don't rush into answering. Start problem-solving out loud. Ask questions, if appropriate.

- If the first response that comes to mind seems too easy, rethink it. There may be a trick to it.

- On the other hand, an apparently complex problem may be simpler than it appears. If it seems to involve higher math, look for an easier solution.

- If you're stuck, examine your assumptions, one by one.

- If there seems to be no one right answer, great! That gives you the opportunity to develop a uniquely creative, memorable one.

The next puzzle will catch you off-guard. Remain calm and don't show any signs of hesitation. Answer affirmatively that you have also heard the puzzle before as well.

The interviewer may be surprised and will not ask for proof, and the bluff will work for you. However, if they go ahead and request the answer, be honest and let them know you were just bluffing and you are not in the know of the correct answer to the puzzle. That may also work in your favor.

The Backup Plan

You may be out of ideas in an interview and the interviewers seem to be bored after looking through your portfolio that does not promise anything. But wait! Before being dismissed, offer some great idea that is beyond your skills. Impress the panel with ideas that you are sure are not ready to do, as long as they are relevant to the career at hand. That backup plan may serve as your winning kick. Go ahead and strike it out.

Chapter 5

Answering Tough Questions

Know What the Interviewer Is Looking for

There are three unspoken questions an interviewer has about you, which you can think of as the **Three C's of Interviewing**. (The following is derived from a model developed by the outplacement firm Lee Hecht Harrison.) The three C's are Competence, Compatibility with the company culture and Chemistry.

Competence: Of course, the interviewer wants to make sure you can do the job, and do it well. This is what we all tend to think the whole interview is about: whether the candidate has the necessary experience, technical skills and soft skills. But actually, there's more.

Compatibility with the company culture: They also want to make sure you'll work well *in this particular environment*, especially if it's quite different from the organizations you've worked in before. For example, some organizations are very hard-driving and competitive while others are more collaborative; some are very hierarchical and formal while others are more open and want everyone to be a leader. Show the employer that you understand and appreciate their company culture and will work well within it. If you have more experience with that type of culture than your resume indicates, clarify that.

Chemistry: Last but not least, they want a sense that you'll "click" with the boss and team members and that they'll enjoy spending a big chunk of their waking hours with you, day after day. Don't underestimate or forget the importance of liking and being liked by the people you're meeting – *all of them*, including the receptionist, shuttle driver and so on. Much of this comes down to everyday things like friendly chitchat, showing an interest in people, active listening and body language such as a firm handshake, eye contact and a warm smile. *In many cases, chemistry is even more important than competence.*

Understand Before You Answer

We've all been taught in school to answer quickly but answering instantly in an interview can give the impression that you're not taking the question seriously, or that you have your answers memorized.

Answering too quickly can also lead to the embarrassing experience of realizing, in the middle of your answer, that you've forgotten the question. So pause for a moment – usually two to five seconds is about right – and repeat the question silently to yourself. If the question is long or complex, repeat it aloud to ensure you've got it right.

While you're at it, make sure you fully *understand* the question. Is it a behavioral question, requiring you to tell a story? Make sure you tell one. Does the question have multiple parts? Get ready to answer them all.

Is the question vague or unclear? Ask for clarification if necessary. "I'd love to answer that, and before I do could you just clarify for me which aspect of ..." This is skillful communication – and it will enable you to give a more relevant answer.

There's another major advantage in asking questions related to what's being discussed: it makes the interview feel more like a dialogue or conversation, and less like an interrogation. That makes it more enjoyable – and a person who enjoyed their conversation with you is more likely to want to work with you.

Listen Between the Lines

Think about what the employer is trying to find out with each question. Usually it's straightforward, as in "Tell me about your experience with (a technique or task)." On the other hand, a question about your boss is indirect: it's really a question about *you*, and whether you're easy to manage, and whether you speak respectfully of others even when they're not present.

Be Specific and Concrete

Question: "What's your management style?" Answer: "I'm fair, my door is always open and I coach my team to excel and help them move up."

This answer sounds trite, uninteresting and vague. It neither informs nor persuades! Why not? Because it lacks the specific details that would make it real and convincing. What do you mean by "fair"? Can you give an example? Do you have a special philosophy or motto about coaching? Can you tell a story about a team member whose career you helped transform?

Keep It Positive

Never volunteer a negative about yourself, such as confessing to a weakness when the interviewer hasn't asked about your weaknesses.

Don't say what you didn't like about any past job, unless asked to do so.

Don't badmouth your former boss, co-workers or company. This is one of the undisputable ways to destroy your chances at a job interview.

Occasionally, a story about your own accomplishments might unavoidably mention challenges created by others: a co-worker not pulling their own weight, or an underperforming employee you managed. Be very tactful, respectful, objective and brief about the behavior. Preserve this person's reputation by omitting any information that would allow anyone to identify them.

***

You may not know all the questions that might be thrown at you during the course of an interview. There are, however, a number of questions that generally crop up and if you read through this chapter you should have a much better appreciation of how to handle them. They will, of course, not come up word for word as they appear in the list below but instead will take on differing guises. Their exact wording is not important. What is important is that once you have read them you can see the reasoning behind them. This will enable you to adapt your own replies and answer with the confidence that will impress the interviewer.

1. Pretend you are our CEO. What three concerns about the firm's future will keep you up at night?

This question gives you a chance to both show that you have really researched the company to whom you are applying, as well as giving you the chance to offer some positive sounding future plans. Don't let it look like you have all the answers or that you are afraid that there are intrinsic problems in the company that really concern you.

2. Why are manhole covers round?

If you happen to be a bit on the rotund side then this is the time to show you have a little humor and can laugh at yourself by suggesting that it allows easier access to rounder physiques like your own. Make sure that you bear the brunt of the joke and do not aim it at overweight city workers. If your physique does not open a door for this sort of humor, then try suggesting that most of the holes are round and so it makes sense to have a cover that fits.

3. What's your favorite song? Perform it for us now.

This question is not to see if you can sing, and 'I Did It My Way' is the wrong answer. On the other hand, 'Love Me Do' by the Beatles might raise a smile and it's easy enough to sing to.

4. Any advice for your previous boss?

You are on dangerous ground here. Pointing out your ex-boss's weak points is not what the interviewer is hoping to see you do. 'Good luck with finding the three new staff you will need to replace me...' might work.

5. How would you resolve problems if you were from Mars?

"I have the technology, intelligence and capability to come all the way from Mars. You are the ones with a problem. How are you going to deal with me?"

6. How would you rate your memory?

"I used to know the answer to that one I'm sure. Can you give me a few minutes to think about it?" Now move in with examples of why your memory is actually good.

7. What's the color of money?

Slightly darker than water but it runs through your fingers more easily.

8. You are a new addition to a crayon box. What color are you?

"A sort of embarrassed red color, but I will pale down to a more typical flesh color when I have become more used to being in this new environment.

9. What do you ponder on when you are alone in your car?

"For the past two weeks I thought about possible questions I might need to be prepared for during this interview. Clearly I did not think broadly enough because that was a question I had not considered. However, I did think of these points to show why I am the ideal candidate...." and then take the floor by presenting some of the reasons you should have the job.

10. How many balloons can fit in this room?

Cast an eye around the room and then ask if the furniture is to be removed first. Whichever way they answer you then reply "11927 providing they were fully inflated." Nobody can argue with you because they have no idea.

11. What is it about yourself that makes you the right candidate for this position?

This question pops up in one form or another

in just about any interview. If the interviewee is not prepared for it they can be left fumbling for words, but if they are prepared it opens the door for them to put their best foot forward and propose, smoothly and elegantly, all the reasons that the job should be theirs. Be careful though. Tone is very important and you should sound confident and knowledgeable, but not come over as being arrogant.

12. Why do you want this job?

This should be a question you have already asked yourself and so it should be easy to roll out a short list of reasons why you have applied for this position. At the same time, you can carefully phrase your answers so that they demonstrate a match between your talents and your reasons for applying for the job. Keep the list short and do not try to impress the interviewer by having the longest list he has ever heard.

13. What strengths do you possess that makes you a good fit for this position?

Again, this is a gift of a question if you have prepared for it. Don't just provide a long list of attributes that you think the employer may be looking for. Pick three or four qualities you may have that are pertinent to the position and expand briefly on each of them.

14. What are your greatest weaknesses?

Another typical question and rarely left out by interviewers, this can be a kind of trap that you create for yourself to fall into. Beware of it. While weaknesses are inherent in humans, you must prepare yourself to present it well and in a dignified manner. Another way of talking about your weakness is telling stories from your past experiences wherein you learnt from your mistakes, and how you have since limited that particular weakness.

Also, when talking about persistent weaknesses, do NOT leave out how you manage and keep these negativities under check and how you ensure that they do not affect your professional life. Having weaknesses is a perfectly natural human trait, but not being aware of them, not accepting them and not planning to keep them under check is clearly unprofessional.

15. What is your greatest professional achievement?

Be careful here. In your working career you will hopefully have done several things that you are proud of. Don't just dive in with the things that pleased you the most. Instead pick the one that would most have benefitted the company that you are applying to now, had you done something similar for them and expand on that.

16. Where do you see yourself in 2/5/10 years?

This is a challenging question. You need to appear ambitious without being unreasonable. Of course if this job is just something you intend to do for a couple of years because you need it on your CV before moving onto bigger things, then don't mention that. Be prepared, if that is the case, for the fact that they may have had other people use the position as a springboard to greater things and be using this as a question to test that you will not quickly be moving on.

17. Tell me about your dream job?

Here is a chance to describe the job you are applying for, and build into it all the positive things you bring with you that match that position.

18. What other companies have you worked for?

They probably already know most of this from looking at your application. This question gives them an opportunity to find out what you did in those companies and your reasons for leaving. Keep everything positive and don't make disparaging remarks about any of the companies that have employed you in the past, even if you had some sort of dispute.

19. Why did you leave your last position?

This often follows the question above. Even if you left your last employer after a stand up shouting match with your boss, keep your answer positive and don't bad mouth the company or anyone that you worked for or with whilst there. Instead, focus more on the idea that you felt you needed to spread your wings more and that you had learned as much as you were going to in the last company but that you had really gained from that learning experience.

20. What work environment most suits you?

Hopefully you know what sort of environment you will be working in through the research that you have done. This is a time to reel off all the things that the new position already offers in the way of a work environment. As an addition, you may throw in one or two new ideas that would bring something positive to the position you are hoping to fill.

21. How can you describe your management style?

As mentioned earlier in the book, each company has its own style and ethic and hopefully you have a clear idea of the style that is already being used. Whilst you need to conform to any boundary that that imposes, you also need to be true to yourself. If the company is a hard-hitting, authoritarian type organization and you have more of a team approach, you might want to word things along the lines of "strict but open to ideas".

22. What is your educational background?

The interviewer will have a basic idea from your CV but now you have been given an open door to expand on that whilst emphasizing what you deem the most positive aspects of your education.

23. Describe yourself?

This trips up so many people who are not expecting the question, but it is a gift for those who are prepared for it. Of course you are not going to say "I am an alcoholic who sleeps late most days and likes to kick his dog after a night on the town." The questioner has just given you a chance to highlight anything constructive about your own character that pertains to the job you are going for. Don't go off tangent by talking about all the good things you did as a Boy Scout but filter down the positive things that would benefit the company if they employed you. Also remember that you have been asked to describe yourself and not just what is positive about yourself. Throw in a few negatives but turn them to positives to demonstrate that you have adopted positive strategies to correct them.

24. What is the name of our CEO?

You better know this one. You should have researched the name of the CEO before the interview begins.

25. What are your hobbies?

This is an easy question that allows you to show something about your personal life. If you aren't involved in a hobby that other people might find interesting, you might want to think about taking one up.

Conclusion

There are any numbers of variations to all interview questions, but if you have ready answers to all of the above then it is unlikely that you will find yourself caught off balance. Hopefully you have learned that preparation and research are fundamental to interview success. The interview is an amalgamation of dress, demeanor, body language and charisma but even should you have been gifted with a natural abundance of all of those things, failure to prepare can let you down.

Thank you and good luck!

Martha Gage